Fill It In & Pass It On

SHARED DIARY SOCIETY
FOR FRIENDS

A Bold & Brave
Question & Answer Book

KATELYN COLE

BETTER DAY BOOKS®

Shared Diary Society for Friends © 2023 by Katelyn Cole
and Better Day Books, Inc.

Publisher: Peg Couch
Book Designer: Lori Ehrlich and Llara Pazdan
Editor: Colleen Dorsey

All rights reserved. No part of this work may be reproduced or
used in any form or by any means — graphic, electronic, or
mechanical, including photocopying or information storage
and retrieval systems — without written permission from the publisher.

"Better Day Books," the floral book logo, and "It's a Good Day to
Have a Better Day" are registered trademarks of Better Day Books, Inc.

"Schiffer," "Schiffer Publishing, Ltd.," and the pen and inkwell logo
are registered trademarks of Schiffer Publishing, Ltd.

Illustrations throughout the book are credited to their respective
creators via Creative Market: "Light Academia," "Dark Academia,"
"Autumn Self-Care," "Botanical Mystery," "Garden and Balcony
Summer Decor," "Lovely Spring Days," "Summer Fashion, Food, and
Leisure," and "Stay Home" packages copyright Ruslana Lubenets;
"Padlocks" package copyright RocketArt. The following art is credited
to its creator via Shutterstock.com: cover plaid by Romance Children.

ISBN: 978-0-7643-6715-1
Printed in China
10 9 8 7 6 5 4 3 2 1

Copublished by Better Day Books, Inc., and Schiffer Publishing, Ltd.

Better Day Books
P.O. Box 21462
York, PA 17402
Phone: 717-487-5523
Email: hello@betterdaybooks.com
www.betterdaybooks.com
@better_day_books

Schiffer Publishing
4880 Lower Valley Road
Atglen, PA 19310
Phone: 610-593-1777
Fax: 610-593-2002
Email: info@schifferbooks.com
www.schifferbooks.com

This title is available for promotional or
commercial use, including special editions.
Contact info@schifferbooks.com
for more information.

[THE BEST THINGS IN LIFE AREN'T THINGS—
they're your friends.]

CONTENTS

Welcome!........................8
How to Use This Book 10
Diary Society Pledge.................12

CHAPTER 1: Our Friendship 15

CHAPTER 2: School 27

CHAPTER 3: Beliefs & Values 39

CHAPTER 4: Hobbies 51

CHAPTER 5: Tough Times...........63

CHAPTER 6: Future 75

CHAPTER 7: Habits & Goals 87

CHAPTER 8: Communication 99

CHAPTER 9: Family & Traditions 111

CHAPTER 10: Emotions 123

CHAPTER 11: Responsibilities 135

CHAPTER 12: Favorite Things.......147

WELCOME!

Welcome to the Diary Society, where there is always something new to learn about your best friend!

A best friendship is a special relationship. There's nothing quite like it! This creative co-journal is a place for you to be open and honest as you take turns responding to questions about your hopes, thoughts, dreams, and fears. Within these pages is a safe space for memories, hard conversations, and laughs, specially designed for the two of you.

This journal is not something to finish in a single day. Rather, it is meant to invite conversations and ignite stories and memories between best friends over time, with the goal of growing your friendship.

Take your time with every page. Take breaks when things get heavy. Laugh a lot! Draw pictures where prompted and play the games as many times as you'd like. Listen to each other and respect each other's honest vulnerability. Some questions will be silly and others will be harder to discuss, but every question is an opportunity to show respect and love for your friend.

This is your space! The two of you get to decide what goes in it. There is no messing it up. You might erase, cross out, and add extra writing in the margins. Remember: this is YOUR journal, and there is no wrong way to do it!

Consider this your permission to let go of perfection and allow your conversations to lead the way. Get ready to take your friendship to a whole new level!

How to Use This Book

This journal can be filled out while you're together or apart—it's up to you! Some of the pages and prompts are specifically designed to be completed while you're together, though, so just save those until you're hanging out.

There are many different kinds of pages in this journal! Some have space for writing long answers to questions; some are focused on straightforward "this or that" or "would you rather" questions; sometimes there's free space to write, draw, and paste photos; and there are even a few games mixed in!

▲ Interactive games to play with your besties

Journal questions to strengthen your bond ▶

As you work through this book, make sure to leave space for your friend to write—don't take up the whole page yourself! Each of you can use a different specific color to write your answers.

If you're really cramped for space because you love to pour your heart out, here's an idea! Whenever you get together with your bud, pick a page and work through it verbally. Just jot down a couple notes on the page as a record of what you talked about.

This book is written for two friends to complete together. However, it's possible for more than two friends to participate! Just leave enough space on the page for everyone's answers.

Before you start, sign the pledge on the next page!

DIARY SOC

BY PARTICIPATING IN THIS
TO FOLLOW THE BYL

I will answer the qu

I will share my thoughts and dream

I will not pressure my friend to a

I will not judge

I will not share our response

I will leave enough s

I will wholeheartedly giv

THIS IS MY DI

Chrissy Torres
SIGNED
11·29·2024

DATE

Y PLEDGE

DIARY, I HEREBY PROMISE
THE DIARY SOCIETY.

this book honestly. ✓
er how big and crazy they may seem. ✓
estion they don't want to answer. ✓
or their answers. ✓
one else without permission. ✓
y friend to write too! ✓
ept the gift of friendship. ✓

IETY PLEDGE.

SIGNED   DATE

CHAPTER 1
OUR FRIENDSHIP

A friendship that makes you feel safe and secure is also the friendship that will make you feel encouraged, inspired, and brave. Being a best friend means being there in the happy times and the hard times.

Growing a deep level of trust in a friendship takes time and effort! Just like a tiny seed doesn't bloom into a flower overnight, a friendship doesn't build trust in a day. Through time, experiences, and vulnerability, you grow to see that your best friend loves you. This chapter is all about opening up conversations. Some will be silly, while others may feel a little more sensitive. Share as much as you feel comfortable, and know that the conversations you have with your best friend are safe here inside your shared diary.

> A best friend knows and protects all your secrets

Start the Conversation

Read the sentence stems below and take turns filling in the answers in the spaces provided. Reflecting on your friendship will help set your mind up for open and honest conversations throughout this journal.

I know I can trust you because . . .

_____
_____

Three words that best describe you are . . .

_____
_____

My favorite memory with you is . . .

_____
_____

Our hardest time together was when . . .

_____
_____

A time I was proud to be your friend was . . .

_____
_____

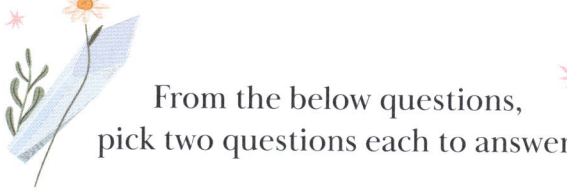

From the below questions,
pick two questions each to answer.

How did we meet?

What is our favorite thing to do together?

What is something that only I know about you?

Whom do you go to for help (besides me)?

What makes our friendship special?

Let's dig a little deeper into what your friendship looks and feels like. Read these journal questions and take turns filling in your answers in the spaces provided.

What did you think of me when we first met?

What are my best qualities?

How can I be a better friend to you?

What is something you have never told me?

What can we do to resolve disagreements?

What song defines our friendship?

Where would we go on a BFF vacation?

If we gave "most likely to" awards to each other, what would they be?

Would You Rather?

Read each scenario. Then, using a different colored pencil for each person, circle your choice in each set of options.

Would you rather live in a hot or cold climate?

Would you rather have a tree house or a swimming pool?

Would you rather be able to breathe underwater or fly?

Would you rather have green or pink hair?

Would you rather grow a garden of vegetables or flowers?

Would you rather be known as funny or helpful?

Would you rather eat only pizza for a year or never eat pizza again?

Would you rather have breakfast for dinner or dinner for breakfast?

Would you rather visit the beach or the mountains?

Would you rather eat the hottest pepper in the world or smell the stinkiest plant in the world?

Would you rather give up your phone for a week or your TV for a month?

Would you rather play video games or go to a live sports game?

Would you rather be able to speak to animals or read human minds?

Would you rather write a book or direct a movie?

Would you rather visit London or Paris?

Would you rather be able to speak every language or remember every book you've ever read?

Would you rather take an ice bath or a hot gravy bath?

Would you rather go back in time or travel to the future?

Would you rather have shark fins for arms or a mermaid tail for legs?

Would you rather repeat your current age for five more years or jump ten years into the future?

Our Friendship | 21

Letter Together

One at a time, use this space to write a short note to each other. Share what you're grateful for in your friendship and any other encouraging comments you have. If you feel more comfortable, write out your messages on pieces of paper and tape them into this space.

Dear _____

Dear

Sometimes, friendship feels so easy! You make memories, encourage each other, share secrets, and try new things. Hopefully, there's lots of laughter throughout these times. If you're lucky, many of your most cherished memories will be together.

Sometimes, though, friendship is hard. You're going to disagree with each other, but that doesn't mean your friendship is over. Disagreement is normal, but try to remember to communicate with respect and care. When you're struggling, come back to this chapter and read your reflections. These are the moments when it's important to remember the value of your friendship.

Before diving further into this journal, go back through your responses in this chapter. Is there anything else you want to add? Any memories, funny moments, or meaningful conversations from today that you want to remember?

OUR FRIENDSHIP, EST. _____

Always changing, always growing— together.

CHAPTER 2
SCHOOL

Navigating the dynamics of school can be challenging at times. Balancing schoolwork and homework, learning new routines, keeping up with multiple teachers and subjects, and forming new friendships are all big tasks. School can also be a source of great joy! It can be a place you feel safe and inspired to learn new things. It can be the place where your greatest memories are made.

One way to make school feel more familiar and comfortable is by understanding how you both feel about it and what you can do to support the other in good times and tough times. It's important to remember whom you can count on when things get stressful. It's important to cherish the great times, so they can help you through the tough times. By understanding how your friendship can be seen and felt at school, you're building a deeper friendship that will last far beyond the school year.

> A best friend is someone you can be an open book with

Start the Conversation

Here is a fun activity to do together! Read the prompts below and take turns filling in the answers in the spaces provided. It's always interesting to see what you each remember most!

Ways I know you care for me at school:

_____
_____

Our favorite memory at school:

_____
_____

Our hardest day at school:

_____
_____

Reasons school is important to us:

_____
_____

Ways we check in with each other at school:

_____
_____

From the questions below,
pick two questions each to answer.

What school subject is your favorite? Why?

What school subject is challenging for you right now?

What is your favorite part of the school day?

What is a goal you have at school?

What do you think are my strengths at school?

Get out your no. 2 pencils! Read these journal questions and take turns filling in your answers in the spaces provided.

What about school makes you happy?

What about school is stressful?

What nonschool subject do you wish you could learn in school?

If you could improve one thing about your school, what would it be?

What is your earliest school memory?

What makes a great teacher?

Whom do you feel comfortable talking to at school (besides me)?

What would you do if you saw someone being treated unkindly at school?

School | 31

This or That?

Using a different colored pencil for each person, circle which of each set of options you would choose! What similarities do you find? What differences surprise you?

Being a student leader
or
being a star athlete

Riding the bus
or
walking to school

Working at your desk
or
working in the library

Going to school at night
or
going to school on the weekend

Social studies
or
home economics

Reading a book alone
or
reading a book in a study group

Reading
or
math

A field trip
or
a day off from school

An extra week of field trips
or
an extra week of summer

Chatting with
friends during
study hall
or
getting your
homework
done first

Music
while you work
or
silence while
you work

A class pet
hamster
or
a school
pet dog

Writing notes
by hand
or
typing notes
on your laptop

Funny friends
or
dependable
friends

Extra
P.E. time
or
extra lunch
time

Organized
desk/locker
or
organized
backpack

Science
or
writing

Music
or
art

Spending
a day in the library
or
spending time
on the field

A packed
lunch from home
or
lunch from the
cafeteria

School | 33

Making Memories

Think about favorite school memories that you both share. Use this space to paste in photos if you have them, or draw them if you don't. Include details that will help you remember why these memories are so special.

If we're being honest, some days at school are absolutely amazing and other days can leave you feeling pretty crummy. A best friend is someone who is there to celebrate the highs with you and comfort you during the lows. Good days and bad days come and go, but your best friend will be there for you no matter what the school day brings.

It's important to know that both of you are not always going to feel the same emotions on the same days. How will you celebrate the highs and comfort the lows for each other? Having open and honest conversations about how your friendship works best at school will ultimately lead to deeper friendship in the long run.

Keep the conversation going! Maybe you don't see much of each other during the school day. How can you still show love and support to each other? Can you walk to class together in the mornings? Can you organize a carpool schedule that allows for conversation and connection after the school day has ended?

NEVER STOP LEARNING

Together forever,

through all chapters
of life.

CHAPTER 3

BELIEFS & VALUES

Talking about values can seem like an overwhelming conversation. Values are personal, and when someone doesn't share the same values as you, it can easily be interpreted as a lack of caring. Often, our values are formed on the basis of our families, traditions, and experiences.

Use this chapter as an opportunity to have deeper conversations. Sharing your passions beyond surface-level conversation is what grows stronger bonds in friendship. Remember, this space is for you to share with openness and listen without judgment.

> A best friend has your back today, tomorrow, and forever

Start the Conversation

Share about the topics that are most important to you by completing the below sentence stems. Opening up about your values will help you build a stronger understanding about each other and help you better grow together as friends!

The most important people in my life are . . .

_____
_____

Someone who encourages me to make a change is . . .

_____
_____

Something I value in my family is . . .

_____
_____

Something I value in my community is . . .

_____
_____

Something I value about the world is . . .

_____
_____

From the questions below, pick two
questions each to answer.

What is an issue in your community that you feel passionately about?

What experience have you had that you greatly value?

What do you believe makes a friendship valuable?

What is something you wish people cared more about?

What is a worldly issue that you feel passionately about?

Beliefs & Values | 41

It can be fun and enlightening to think about and reflect on theoretical situations as well as simply think about what we personally value in life. Read these journal questions and take turns filling in your answers in the spaces provided.

Can money buy happiness?

How do you show your loved ones that you care about them?

If you could create a group to make a change, what would it be for?

What do you value about yourself?

What is my best quality?

Is it ever okay to lie?

What is a memory we have together that you value?

If you could spend the day with anyone, living or deceased, who would it be?

Would You Rather?

Read each scenario. Then, using a different colored pencil for each person, circle your choice in each set of options.

Would you rather have one million dollars or one million memories?

Would you rather donate money to a children's hospital or volunteer at an animal shelter?

Would you rather live in a world without hate or without poverty?

Would you rather go on a vacation or save the money it would cost?

Would you rather have a family movie night at home or a family dinner at a restaurant?

Would you rather spend the day reading or hiking?

Would you rather give a gift or get a gift?

Would you rather speak a new language or learn to play a new instrument?

Would you rather have a perfect day but no one to share it with or a day of mistakes with a friend to share it?

Would you rather start a school campaign to increase recycling or to reduce bullying?

Would you rather give up electronics or junk food?

 Would you rather participate in a community garden or plant a garden of your own?

 Would you rather pick up trash in the park or collect canned food for the community food pantry?

 Would you rather donate your time or your money?

 Would you rather cook meals or collect warm clothing for those in need?

 Would you rather cook a meal for your family or help clean the house?

 Would you rather be the best player on a losing team or the worst player on a winning team?

 Would you rather give up your phone or TV?

 Would you rather be known as a funny friend or an honest friend?

Would you rather live in the country or a city?

Be the Change

At this point, you've probably discovered that you both have some similar values and some different ones. Use this space to compile a collection of topics that you each value. Brainstorm some ways you could work together to make a positive change in your school, community, and even the world!

It's important to remember that you can have different values and still be friends. Each of you has values instilled in you from your families, experiences, and communities that make you unique. When talking about values and choices, you probably recognized that each of you has some values that the other does not.

Do you have any questions about your friend's values? Did you learn anything new about each other? What would you like to know more about?

See these differences as opportunities to share and grow. How can you support each other's differing passions? How can you learn from each other's values? Remember that working together creates a stronger impact than working alone.

IT'S OKAY TO BE DIFFERENT

CHAPTER 4

HOBBIES

Hobbies are important experiences that can help you relax or bring you excitement. Having interest in a hobby not only can bring you joy but also teach you valuable skills along the way. A healthy hobby will bring you a mix of peace and inspiration!

One of the things that makes having a best friend so special is spending time together! Sharing your hobbies and trying new ones together are great ways to make memories. Some hobbies come naturally, and some take hard work and practice. Take this time to share the activities you love and get inspired to try some new hobbies together!

> A best friend will drop anything to do nothing with you

Start the Conversation

Use the below prompts to spark conversations about your favorite hobbies! This will be a special chapter to look back on and remember your favorite things to do both together and separately.

One activity we love doing together:

_____
_____

Hobbies I enjoy that you don't:

_____
_____

A way I can support your hobby:

_____
_____

Something I would like us to try together:

_____
_____

Ways we can find the courage to try new things:

_____
_____

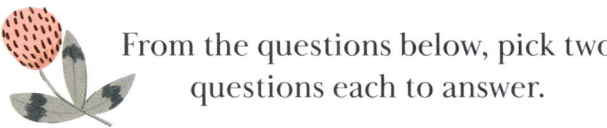

From the questions below, pick two questions each to answer.

What indoor activity do you enjoy?

What outdoor activity do you enjoy?

Have you ever wanted to give up on a hobby?

Who inspired you to start doing your hobby?

What makes your hobby enjoyable?

Think further than just the enjoyment you get from your hobbies as you read these journal questions and take turns filling in your answers.

What new skill would you like to learn?

How do you keep yourself motivated when a skill is difficult to learn?

What does it take to learn a new hobby?

What makes your hobby special for you?

What is something that is really difficult for you?

What is something that you could teach others how to do?

Do you have any collections?

How does trying something new make you feel?

This or That?

Using a different colored pencil for each person, circle which hobby or activity each of you would choose!

Going shopping
or
going to a movie theater

Journaling
or
coloring

Drawing
or
hand lettering

Video games
or
watching YouTube

Soccer
or
baseball

Traveling
or
a staycation

Volleyball
or
golf

Volunteering
or
photography

Doing puzzles
or
dancing

Playing sports
or
watching them

A nature walk
or
painting

Camping
or
glamping

Playing an instrument
or
cooking

An amusement park
or
a zoo

Gardening
or
riding a bike

Running
or
swimming

Books
or
movies

Football
or
basketball

Yoga
or
cheerleading

Board games
or
card games

Hobbies | 57

Hobbies to Discover

Hobbies help us grow and teach us valuable lessons that we can use throughout life. On this spread, you'll find an assortment of different hobbies—some of which you may already do, and some of which you don't! Pick three hobbies to try together.

Collect records

Try a new exercise routine

Learn to knit

Start a gratitude diary

Take up baking

Start a new sport

Start a garden

Go camping

Volunteer at an animal shelter

Give your space a makeover

Take an online course

Having a shared hobby is a great way to bond with your best friend. Participating in an activity that you both enjoy offers opportunities for stronger communication, shared experiences, and encouraging each other's growth. It's also important to embrace each other's hobbies! You can support your friend by attending one of their sporting events or offering to spend time with them doing their hobby.

Look back at the first part of this chapter. What activity would you like to try together? Do you prefer calming hobbies like painting or reading, or do you prefer fast-paced activities like soccer or bike riding? Make a plan to try something new together! This is the perfect opportunity to encourage, support, and laugh with each other.

It's normal to feel vulnerable and nervous when trying something new, but the best part is having a friend who is right there with you. Learn, make memories, and laugh together!

DOUBLE YOUR FUN WITH A FRIEND

Better together.
Besties forever.

CHAPTER 5

TOUGH TIMES

Friendship is easiest in the happy times, but it's the tough times that truly show your friendship in action. Tough times are guaranteed—everyone has them! What makes the tough times more bearable is having a friend to be a listening ear, a shoulder to cry on, and a voice of encouragement.

This chapter may be difficult at times. Talk as openly with each other as you feel comfortable, and remember the commitment you made at the beginning of this journal. This space is for both of you to confide in one another and to feel confident in each other's trust!

A best friend makes you laugh when you feel like crying

Start the Conversation

Use the below prompts to begin your conversation on tough times. These might be hard topics to talk about. Speak with care and trust. If you don't feel comfortable sharing, it's okay to come back to this section at another time.

A time I felt scared:

_____
_____

A time I felt sad:

_____
_____

A time I felt worried:

_____
_____

A time I felt angry:

_____
_____

A strategy I used to calm myself:

_____
_____

If you feel comfortable, keep going.
Together, pick three questions to answer.

How comfortable do you feel telling someone when they have hurt your feelings?

What is the difference between feeling sad and feeling worried?

How do you move past being angry with someone?

Besides me, who do you trust to talk to during a tough time?

What can we do for each other when we are having a tough time?

Think more deeply about past tough experiences and the ways you deal with them. Read these journal questions and take turns filling in your answers in the spaces provided.

What is the hardest emotion for you to process?

What is most worrying to you about the world right now?

What is the hardest thing about being a kid?

How have tough times helped you grow?

Have we had any tough times where we were at odds with each other?

How do we work through disagreements with each other?

Have we gone through any tough times together?

Are there any tough times you want to talk about now?

Would You Rather?

Read each scenario. Then, using a different colored pencil for each person, circle your choice in each set of options.

Would you rather write a letter or talk face to face?

Would you rather forgive and forget or forgive and remember?

Would you rather have a difficult conversation with a friend or just pretend everything is fine?

Would you rather get advice from a friend or a parent?

Would you rather go on a walk or listen to music to calm yourself down?

Would you rather have a little homework each night or lots of homework but only on one night?

Would you rather be bored with nothing to do or have a fully booked schedule of activities?

Would you rather practice mindfulness with yoga or with breathing techniques?

Would you rather be sad alone or with a friend?

Would you rather get a great night's sleep or eat a full breakfast?

Would you rather give up media or after-school activities?

 Would you rather admit that something is your fault or keep it to yourself?

 Would you rather work alone or with a group?

 Would you rather talk or be alone when you are upset?

Would you rather have no internet or no cell phone?

 Would you rather have a group of friends you have to fit into or be fully yourself and have just one friend?

 Would you rather keep a journal of your thoughts or record a podcast?

 Would you rather share your things with a sibling or never share at all?

Would you rather face your fear or never have to face your fear?

 Would you rather reach out for help or wait for someone to offer it?

Self-Care Ideas

This chapter may have been difficult for you. When times are tough, turn to self-care to stay sane and healthy. On these pages you'll find ideas for self-care that you can try out alone or with your friend. Add your own ideas too!

Call a friend

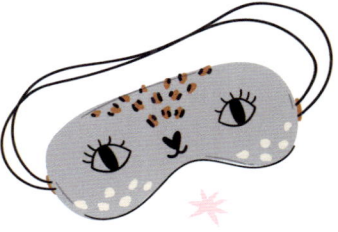

Get a good night's sleep

Listen to your favorite music

Try aromatherapy

Take care of houseplants

Get some vitamin D

Try a new self-care product

Go for a bike ride

Sip on a hot drink

Put on your coziest PJs

Take a bubble bath

Life will bring hard times. You'll have disagreements. You'll experience disappointment. You'll feel worry and sadness. These times are not necessarily fun, but there is much to gain from them. Understanding that tough times happen to everyone can help you feel less alone.

Sharing your struggles with a trusted friend or family member can be a great way to process what you're going through. Sometimes you find a solution, and other times you just need a listening ear. It's important to recognize that the weight you carry will be lightened when you share it with someone you trust.

When your friend is going through a tough time, it can be hard to know what to do. One question you can ask is "Do you want me to listen or do you want me to help fix the problem?" This will help your friend to feel heard and know that you are ready to help in a way that feels right to them!

> YOU ARE NOT ALONE

Through thick or thin,
count me in.

CHAPTER 6

FUTURE

How do you feel when you think about your future? Excited? A little scared? Unsure? Maybe you've never taken the time to think about what you want in the future. Use this chapter as a launching point for your dreams.

There is something magical in thinking about the future! Dreaming doesn't require a firm plan or a commitment. That's the beauty of it. Anything is possible! Dream big and share your hopes, even if it feels silly. Speaking your hopes and dreams out loud (and writing them down) is a powerful first step toward making your dreams a reality.

> A best friend believes in your dreams as much as you do

Start the Conversation

Dreaming about the future is so exciting! Anything is possible. Use the below prompts to share your hopes and dreams with each other.

Something that excites me about the future:

_____
_____

A dream I have for my future:

_____
_____

Something I hope we do together in the future:

_____
_____

What I hope to look back on in my life when I'm older:

_____
_____

How I see us in the future:

_____
_____

Choose a question at random and answer it.
Repeat until all questions have been answered.

What future experiences do you think will make you happy?

How do you think the world will be different in the future?

If you could make a positive world change to the future, what would it be?

When you think about your future, who do you hope is there?

Do you have any big wishes for the future?

Sharing your hopes for the future with a close friend builds trust. Keep the conversation going with the below questions.

What is something you would like to accomplish in the next year?

What activities and clubs would you like to try in high school?

Do you plan to go to college?

What types of jobs are you interested in?

Where would you like to live someday?

What do you hope you are like in 10 years?

Where would you like to travel?

What do you hope our friendship is like in the future?

This or That?

Using a different colored pencil for each person, circle which future job each of you would choose!

Astronaut
or
choreographer

Car mechanic
or
electrician

Event planner
or
farmer

Engineer
or
meteorologist

Author
or
musician

App creator
or
YouTuber

Chef
or
secret agent

Firefighter
or
mayor

Teacher
or
business owner

Aesthetician (beautician) **or** paleontologist

Artist **or** travel blogger

Scientist **or** painter

Doctor **or** veterinarian

Actor **or** police officer

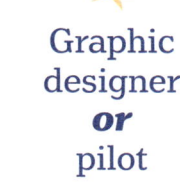
Graphic designer **or** pilot

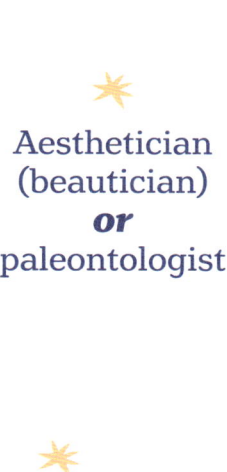

Lawyer **or** bookshop owner

Babysitter **or** dog walker

Florist **or** librarian

Journalist **or** marine biologist

Pro athlete **or** architect

Unlocking Your Future

Who will save the world with amazing new inventions? Who will find themselves surrounded by babies and a big family? Who will be an adventurous traveler? Read the prompts and decide which person you think is the most likely to do each thing. Write the person's name next to the prompt and have fun comparing answers.

 Most likely to live to 100

 Most likely to go viral online

 Most likely to save the world

 Most likely to stand up for what's right

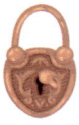 Most likely to be remembered for their kindness

 Most likely to become a millionaire

 Most likely to open a bakery

 Most likely to start a fashion trend

 Most likely to become a household name

 Most likely to own the absolute coolest car

 Most likely to invent something

 Most likely to make a lot of speeches

 Most likely to speak at least four languages

 Most likely to spend a lot of time on the road

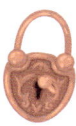 Most likely to live on a farm surrounded by animals

 Most likely to become an interior designer

 Most likely to rule the world

 Most likely to visit 100 countries

 Most likely to stay in touch

 Most likely to become a pop star

 Most likely to have a big family

 Most likely to break a world record

 Most likely to have their artwork in a museum

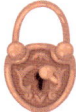 Most likely to publish a book

This chapter may have led you to thinking about some new ideas. It's okay if you weren't sure about some of the answers. It's okay for your hopes and dreams to change, too, as you grow and change. Giving thought to your hopes and dreams will help guide you on your path.

The purpose of sharing your desires for the future is to allow yourself the opportunity to start thinking about what inspires and excites you. Having a best friend to share your dreams with can be comforting and encouraging! As you come to realize your dreams, keep sharing them with your trusted friend.

Think about the conversations you had through this chapter. Did you learn anything new about your best friend? Do you have similar dreams? What about your futures may be different, and how can you keep supporting each other on your paths to achieving your dreams?

DREAM THE IMPOSSIBLE

CHAPTER 7
HABITS & GOALS

Creating healthy habits for our minds and bodies keeps us feeling our best. The same can be said for eliminating negative habits we've developed. We feel better and have more energy to focus on positive choices when we work to break habits that hold us back.

One of the best perks of having a best friend is having a built-in accountability partner! Setting goals for yourself can feel intimidating and may make you feel unsure of where to begin. A friend who can help you plan progress and encourage you along the way will help you stick with your goals.

> A best friend tells you the truth, even when you don't want to hear it

Start the Conversation

Let's begin with habits! Habits, both good and bad, are repeated behaviors that either enhance your life or make it more difficult. Get to understand your friend's habits better by responding to the prompts below.

A good habit I'm proud of:

_____
_____

A good habit I would like to form:

_____
_____

A bad habit I've broken:

_____
_____

A bad habit I would like to break:

_____
_____

A healthy habit I think is important:

_____
_____

Small habits can work together to help you accomplish big goals! Look at the questions below and determine what goals, if any, you've set for yourself in the past and how you can support each other moving forward.

What is a goal you have for yourself this month?

What is a goal you have for yourself this year?

What will it take to reach your goals?

How can we support each other to achieve our goals?

What is a goal we could accomplish together?

Let's get a little more specific about habits and goals! Take turns answering the questions below and set a goal together.

What talents or special abilities do you have?

How did you learn those talents?

What previous goals have you accomplished?

What is a goal you have at school?

What are three qualities it takes to reach your goals?

What advice would give your younger self on working toward your goals?

If you could make everyone form one healthy habit, what would it be?

Set a new goal right now! For example: Do something kind for another person once per week.

Would You Rather?

Read each scenario. Then, using a different colored pencil for each person, circle your choice in each set of options.

Would you rather wake up early or sleep in?

Would you rather eat a quick breakfast or cook a large breakfast?

Would you rather pack your lunch or buy lunch at school?

Would you rather read or practice a sport every day?

Would you rather give up junk food or sodas?

Would you rather take a walk or go for a bike ride?

Would you rather do homework as soon as you get home or after dinner?

Would you rather go to sleep at the same time every night or when you're ready?

Would you rather save your allowance or spend it?

Would you rather have great sportsmanship or perfect table manners?

Would you rather talk about your goals or keep them to yourself?

Would you rather fold laundry or unload the dishwasher?

 Would you rather track your progress in a journal or on a chart?

 Would you rather read 100 books or learn a new language?

 Would you rather exercise or eat healthy foods every day?

 Would you rather Facetime or text a relative?

 Would you rather have several small goals or one large goal?

 Would you rather learn how to dunk a basketball or grow a garden?

 Would you rather learn a dance or complete a 1,000-piece puzzle?

 Would you rather beat a video game or learn to cook a new recipe?

GAME: Spinning the Future

To play this game, you'll need a paper clip and a pencil. Create a spinner with the paper clip by holding it in place on this book page (at the center of the spinner board) using the pencil. Take turns spinning the paper clip. Where it lands, complete the sentence with your own goals for the future!

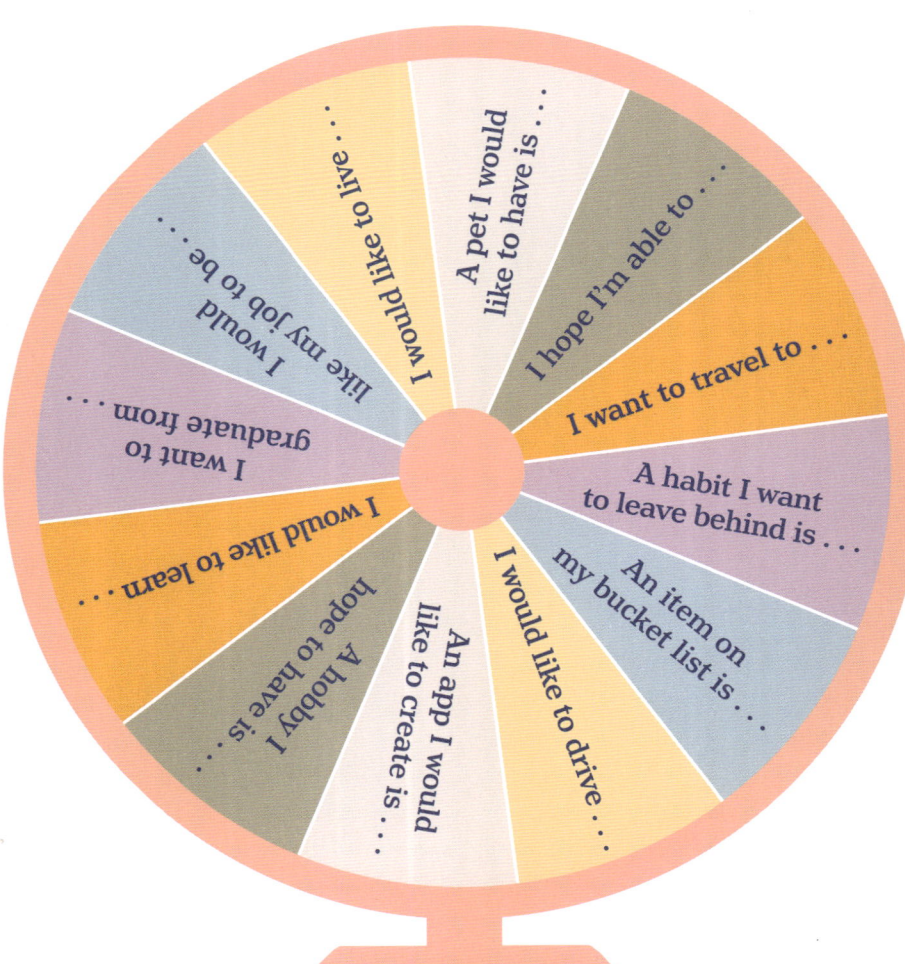

Play as many times as you'd like, and see if you can land on all of the questions. Record your answers on this page.

SPIN 1

SPIN 2

SPIN 3

SPIN 4

SPIN 5

SPIN 6

SPIN 7

SPIN 8

SPIN 9

SPIN 10

SPIN 11

SPIN 12

Sharing your habits and goals may have made you feel timid or nervous. It can be hard to discuss bad habits you're not proud of or good habits you haven't yet created. Forming habits doesn't happen overnight. They take time and repetition, which is why sharing your goals with a friend is so important!

Sharing your struggles and goals with a trusted friend allows you to support and encourage each other. Sticking with your commitment to form healthy habits or reach a goal will inevitably be hard at times. You may feel discouraged and tempted to quit. These are the times when you can support your best friend by reminding them of why they wanted to accomplish that goal and encouraging them to stay committed!

A commonly used goal-setting strategy is to break a big goal into smaller, more easily achievable goals. For example, if your goal is to read 100 books in a year, break it down to smaller goals of 8 or 9 books a month or even 2 books a week! As you make progress, keep a record so that you can see how much you've accomplished.

ONE STEP AT A TIME

You count on me, and
I'll count on you.

CHAPTER 8
COMMUNICATION

Having strong communication skills not only will help you in your future but will also allow you to grow deeper friendships right here and now! Learning how to best communicate with each other during times of sadness, stress, and happiness takes practice. Everyone communicates differently!

Think about a time when your friend was upset. What did you say and what nonverbal things did you do to show you care? This chapter is meant to help you understand how to best communicate when things get hard as well as when things are going great.

> A best friend knows what you're thinking with just one look

Start the Conversation

Let's start by simply opening up to one another about your relationship by completing the below sentence stems. Getting the important words out is half the battle for successful communication!

I know I can trust you because . . .

_____
_____

You show me you care by . . .

_____
_____

It meant a lot to me when you . . .

_____
_____

A difficult time in our friendship was . . .

_____
_____

The maddest I ever saw you was . . .

_____
_____

From the questions below, pick two
questions each to answer.

What do you think is the most challenging conversation we've ever had?

What is something that only I know?

Are you more of a talker or a listener?

When you are upset, how would you like me to help?

Is there anything you want to tell me now but are afraid to?

Examining what makes each of you unique can help shed light on how each of you communicates. Read these journal questions and take turns filling in your answers in the spaces provided.

What three words best describe your friend?

What good things do you have to say about your friend?

What makes your friend unique?

When is a time you were proud of your friend?

What is something people often misunderstand about your friend?

What is your friend's pet peeve?

What are three things we can do when we disagree?

What are three things we can do to celebrate our friendship?

This or That?

Using a different colored pencil for each person, circle your communication preferences. Remember, not all communication has to be verbal!

Celebrating accomplishments with a meal
or
with an activity

Talking it out
or
writing it out

Going to the zoo
or
getting your nails done

Talking about feelings
or
talking about the future

Writing a kind note
or
giving a gift

Crying alone
or
crying with a friend

Giving advice
or
receiving it

Talking on the phone
or
texting

Sharing your opinion
or
going with what your friend says

Talking
right away after
a disagreement
or
taking a break
first

Asking
for help
or
keeping your
problems to
yourself

Speaking
first
or
listening
first

Hanging
with a big group
of friends
or
a small group
of friends

Team games
or
independent
games

Going to a
movie
or
playing a
game

A photo album
or
a video of
memories

Baking
a cake
or
taking a
walk

Facetime
or
Zoom

Making a
birthday card
or
making a birthday
cake

Spending
lunch together
or
hanging out after
school

Communication | 105

GAME: Flip for Questions

You'll need a coin to play this game. Taking turns, flip a coin into the air and try to land it on one of the question cards on these pages.

Talk about a time that technology caused you stress or difficulty.

Talk about a time you faced peer pressure and how you handled it.

Talk about how our communication is different with each other than with other people.

Talk about the importance of privacy and if you've ever felt your privacy was violated.

Talk about learning to work well with others and the pros and cons of doing so.

Talk about homework and whether or not it should be assigned.

Read the prompt and have a conversation about the topic. Do this for at least three of the prompts. If you want to make this game competitive, name the question card you're trying to land on before you flip the coin, and score a point if you manage to land on it!

Talk about feeling understood and how your friends and family make you feel.

Talk about a time you caused harm to someone else and what you did to make amends.

Talk about saying "no" and if you've ever felt it was difficult to tell someone no.

Talk about free time and how you like to spend it.

Talk about your family and experiences you've had with them.

Talk about school and your general feelings about it.

Communicating with your friend in a way that shows them love, care, and respect is a skill that will develop over time. Keep the conversation open. If you would like your friend to support you in a certain way, tell them. You should also be asking you friend how you can best support them in different times of need.

There will be plenty of fun times and memories that you'll make. Cherish them! There will also be times of disagreement, sadness, and anger. In those moments, you may feel at a loss for words. You might not yet know how to express your emotions. It's okay to pause and regroup before continuing communication.

The most important thing to remember is not to give up the friendship during a time of stressful communication. As you both grow, you'll get better at understanding what the other needs. You'll get better at communicating what you need to. The key is trust!

WHEN IN DOUBT, TALK IT OUT

CHAPTER 9
FAMILY & TRADITIONS

Families and their traditions are unique! No two families are exactly alike. Your families may have similarities, perhaps even similarities that led you to becoming friends. Or your families may be very different! Differences are an opportunity to show your friend what influences and traditions are important to your family.

In this chapter, you'll share what makes your families special. Do you have weekly or yearly traditions? Do you celebrate different holidays? Take this time to get to know each other's families even better!

> A best friend will answer your call, even in the middle of the night

Start the Conversation

Let's start by identifying some traits of your families. Use these prompts to help kick off conversations!

One way our families are similar:

_____
_____

One way our families are different:

_____
_____

Something I love about my family:

_____
_____

One thing I want you to know about my family:

_____
_____

Three words to describe my family:

_____
_____

Keep the conversation going by
answering these questions in any order!

- What is your favorite family tradition?

- Do you wish you could spend more time with any family members?

- How is your family different from other families?

- What is a lesson you have learned from your family?

- How does your family show love?

Share a few more details on how your family is unique. These questions may spark memories or new conversations. It's okay to go off topic! Sometimes the most meaningful conversations are unplanned.

What pet do you wish your family had?

Who is the person you are most like or unlike in your family?

What activities does your family often do together?

Has your family ever moved? Was it a positive or negative experience?

Has your family taken any memorable vacations?

What is one thing you would change about your family?

What are your family's favorite foods?

If you could have a celebrity join your family, who would it be?

Would You Rather?

Read each scenario. Then, using a different colored pencil for each person, circle your choice in each set of options.

Would you rather be the oldest kid or the youngest kid in your family?

Would you rather live with your extended family or just your closest family members?

Would you rather have a family game night or a family paint night?

Would you rather take a family cruise or visit New York City together?

Would you rather give birthday gifts or handmade birthday cards?

Would you rather do all the cooking or all the cleaning?

Would you rather have matching family pajamas or cook a meal together on holidays?

Would you rather your family go to the movies every Friday or a restaurant every Saturday?

Would you rather be completely responsible for a family pet or not have a pet at all?

Would you rather share a room with a sibling or live with your friend?

Would you rather your family volunteer once a month or go on family walks every week?

 Would you rather have a secret family handshake or bury a time capsule together?

 Would you rather stay at your grandparents' house or trade places with your best friend for a week?

 Would you rather have a small allowance and few chores or a bigger allowance and more chores?

 Would you rather have a family talent show or a family interview?

 Would you rather make a family scrapbook or start a family gratitude jar?

 Would you rather make a new rule at your house or eliminate an existing rule?

 Would you rather go camping or apple picking as a family?

 Would you rather take family photos or plant a garden together each year?

 Would you rather have complete freedom and no allowance or a big allowance but lots of rules?

Your family and the unique traditions you have with them are special. It may make you feel vulnerable to share about the routines and traditions your family has. But it is often traditions like cooking together on holidays and movie nights that bond your family and make memories you'll carry forever.

When you allow your friend to share in those experiences with you, you open up a piece of your life that is near to your heart. Consider letting your friend join you in a family tradition! This experience will deepen your trust and build a stronger friendship.

Are there any traditions you and your friend would like to start together? Think about a shared experience or activity that you could do to start a tradition of your own!

EMBRACE & SHARE TRADITIONS

Our lives and memories are woven together.

CHAPTER 10

EMOTIONS

A friendship that makes you feel safe enough to share your emotions freely is one to cherish closely! What makes you feel comfortable sharing your emotions with your friend, rather than a stranger or acquaintance, is the trust and respect you build over time.

As you journal together, keep in mind the things you discussed in the Communication chapter. Being vulnerable about emotions helps you understand each other on a deeper level, but it does take time. Be mindful and kind when discussing your emotions. Know that it's okay not to talk about something that makes you feel very uncomfortable, but you should challenge yourself to push through a little discomfort!

> A best friend loves you even when you're struggling to love yourself

Start the Conversation

To your level of comfort, share about your emotions by completing these sentence stems.

I'm grateful for you because . . .

_____
_____

A time I felt frustrated with you was . . .

_____
_____

I was worried when you . . .

_____
_____

One of my favorite times with you was . . .

_____
_____

Our friendship makes me feel . . .

_____
_____

Stay open to learning more about your friend's emotions. Choose one or two of the below questions that you feel comfortable answering.

What does it feel like when you are anxious?

What do you do when you're mad?

Has your friend ever hurt your feelings? Do you want to talk about it?

How does it feel when you are happy?

How do you recognize when you are getting upset?

Share about your emotions in action!
Answer the below questions by reflecting on some recent experiences.

What emotion do you feel most days?

What emotions do you usually feel at home?

Whom are you missing right now?

What is something that confuses you right now?

What was your favorite part of this past week?

What was the hardest part of this past week?

What is one thing that always makes you feel better?

What is the biggest way I can help you when you are upset?

This or That?

Using a different colored pencil for each person, circle your preferences for calming down and de-stressing.

Listening to a playlist of favorite songs
or
shuffling your favorite artist

Facing a fear
or
writing about it

Playing a video game
or
watching funny cat videos

Going shopping
or
painting your nails

Breathing exercises
or
stretches

Reading a physical book
or
listening to an audiobook

Writing a letter to yourself
or
talking with a friend

Going stargazing
or
making a fairy garden

Staying up late
or
sleeping in

Making a
list of things
you're good at
or
writing a letter
to your future
self

Inviting a
friend over
or
meeting them
at the park

Drawing
or
coloring

Walking
barefoot in
the grass
or
in the sand

Talking
with a teacher
or
with a
counselor

A fruit
bowl
or
a smoothie

Using a
daily journal
or
a mood
tracker

Animal
therapy
or
art therapy

Meditating
or
taking a
long walk

Rereading
your favorite book
or
rewatching your
favorite movie

Spending
time in nature
or
listening to
music

Don't Bottle It Up!

Expressing emotions helps you work through them. Think about a time when you experienced a very strong positive emotion (such as joy, surprise, or love) and a time when you experienced a very strong negative emotion (such as hopelessness, grief, or anger). Use this space to write out how you felt. Be open and honest.

Let it out—
it's healthy to
express emotions

Processing emotions looks different for everyone. The first step in learning to process your emotions is to identify what you're feeling. Once you understand how you're feeling, you can better express it to someone you trust.

It's powerful to be able to express your emotions to a friend. Often, when a friend comes to you with their emotions, they aren't looking for you to fix the problem—they just want to feel heard and understood. Being a listening ear is a powerful element of friendship.

As your friendship grows, you're going to experience highs and lows together and separately. Encourage each other to talk through your emotions. Remember to keep an open mind and a calm heart when discussing disagreements.

IT'S OKAY TO FEEL YOUR FEELINGS

CHAPTER 11

RESPONSIBILITIES

Getting older means more freedoms, but it also means more responsibilities. Responsibilities at school, at home, with siblings, and in extracurricular activities all grow as you get older. Some of these responsibilities are ones you'll seek out; others will fall on your shoulders whether you want them or not.

Sometimes, your responsibilities may feel overwhelming. You'll find strength and connection in sharing your experiences with your friend. Everyone goes through this kind of growth. Use this chapter to share responsibilities—not literally, but emotionally!

> A best friend adds sparkle to an ordinary day

Start the Conversation

Let's start by talking about the kinds of responsibilities you have in your lives.

Three responsibilities you have:

_____

_____

A responsibility you like:

_____

_____

A responsibility you struggle with:

_____

_____

Something that motivates you to do your best:

_____

_____

Something I'm proud of you for:

_____

_____

From the questions below, pick two
questions each to answer.

How do you feel about your current responsibilities?

If you could trade responsibilities with someone, who would it be?

Do you have commitments outside school and home?

How do you manage your responsibilities?

Do you feel responsibilities toward your friends?

Keep it simple

Dig deeper into responsibilities and obligations by reading these journal questions and filling in your answers.

What is something you've done to make someone else's day easier?

If you could invent a tool to do a job for you, what would it be?

What responsibilities do you have at school?

What responsibilities do you have at home?

If you had a secret responsibility, what would it be?

If you could start a club with your friends, what would it be?

If you had three wishes, what would they be?

What is one home responsibility you wish you could eliminate?

Would You Rather?

Read each scenario. Then, using a different colored pencil for each person, circle your choice in each set of options.

Would you rather change the bedsheets or clean the bathroom?

Would you rather walk the dog or rake the leaves?

Would you rather babysit or dogsit?

Would you rather eat fruits or vegetables?

Would you rather dust the house or wash the dishes?

Would you rather prepare a week of lunches ahead of time or pack a new lunch every day?

Would you rather take out the trash or feed your pet?

Would you rather invite a new student to eat lunch with you or to sit with you in class?

Would you rather sell lemonade or have a bake sale?

Would you rather work on a group project or work alone?

Would you rather have a house that cleans itself or homework that does itself?

Would you rather paint your room a new color or get all new furniture?

Would you rather do homework during free time at school or at home?

Would you rather take an advanced academic class or an additional elective class?

Would you rather clean your bedroom or vacuum the house?

Would you rather keep a paper schedule or a digital schedule?

Would you rather have school four longer days a week or five shorter days a week?

Would you rather budget and save your allowance or spend it each week?

Would you rather do all your chores on one day or do one chore every day?

Would you rather mow the grass or pull weeds from the garden?

GAME: Roll a Responsibility

To play this game, you'll need one die. Take turns rolling the die and answering the question that corresponds to the number that you rolled. Reroll if you've already answered both questions for that number. If you want to make the game competitive, add up the die value every time each person answers a question, and stop when one winner hits 20 points!

Tell your favorite meal to cook
or
Share your favorite restaurant to visit

Tell your favorite chore
or
Share your favorite reward

Tell about a time you volunteered
or
Share a time when you did something helpful for another person

Tell how you like to spend your allowance
or
Share a time when you felt recognized
for your hard work

Tell about an activity you like doing
after school
or
Share your favorite weekend activity

Tell something you wish you didn't have to do
or
Share something you would like
to be allowed to do

Responsibilities are a part of growing up. Sometimes it will feel empowering to be trusted with new tasks, and other times your responsibilities will feel like burdens. A positive perspective will keep you feeling grateful. Rather than seeing your responsibilities as hardships, reframe your mindset to see them as opportunities to show maturity and growth.

One way you may plan out your responsibilities is with a calendar or an agenda. Using a tool like an agenda will help you keep different areas of your life organized. You can simply make a daily to-do list for yourself or buy a cool agenda.

If you feel like your responsibilities are more than you can handle, reach out for help! Managing responsibilities is a learned skill that takes practice. Do you need help in any areas of responsibility?

IT'S OKAY TO ASK FOR HELP

CHAPTER 12

FAVORITE THINGS

This final chapter is all about celebrating what makes you YOU! Each of you has your own likes and dislikes, characteristics, and passions. You have similarities and differences that all blend together to make your unique friendship!

Spend some time documenting all your favorites! Let this chapter be a time capsule for this moment in your friendship. Your favorites may change over time. You'll be able to look back and remember what you valued most right now!

> A best friend knows what you're going to order before you do!

Start the Conversation

Start off by sharing your feelings! Take turns finishing the sentence stems below.

My favorite memory is . . .

_____

_____

I'm happiest when . . .

_____

_____

I'm really good at . . .

_____

_____

I love that my best friend . . .

_____

_____

One way I've grown is . . .

_____

_____

Keep the conversation going! Take turns
answering each of the below questions.

How would you decorate your future house?

If you could have dinner with a celebrity, who would it be?

If you could time travel, where would you go?

What emoji best describes you?

What is your favorite app or website?

Favorite Things

Favorites change over time as you collect new experiences. Use this space to share your current favorites in each category. See how many change in six months or a year!

What is your favorite smell? What does it evoke for you?

What is your favorite way to spend a Sunday afternoon?

What is your favorite place? Why do you love it?

What is your favorite animal? Why?

What is your favorite music? What does it do to your mood?

What is your favorite game? Why do you love playing it?

What is your favorite book? What about it do you love?

What is your favorite movie? How does it make you feel?

This or That?

Using a different colored pencil for each person, circle which of each set of options you would choose!

Fast food
or
home-cooked meals

Mountains
or
beaches

Sunshine
or
rain

Word searches
or
sudoku

Hair loose
or
hair styled

Jeans
or
leggings

Sweet
or
sour

Cookes
or
cake

Movie theater
or
arcade

In-person school
or
VR school

Appetizers
or
desserts

Snow
or
heat

Sunsets
or
stargazing

Jokes
or
riddles

Inside
or
outside

Live music
or
playlsts

Yellow
or
green

Pizza
or
sushi

Tennis shoes
or
sandals

Earbuds
or
headphones

Favorite Things | 153

GAME: Follow the Faves

You'll need a die and two small objects for this game. Roll the die and move your object the corresponding number of spaces along the path. State your favorite for the prompt on that space. Take turns until someone has reached the finish line—they have to land exactly on the FINISH space. Repeat the game as many times as you'd like!

Friendship grows from tiny moments of connection over an extended amount of time. You share jokes, secrets, wishes, emotions, and trust. Having different favorites doesn't mean you have nothing in common—it just means you have more opportunities to share in each other's enjoyment!

Memories are made through new experiences. Sharing in your friend's favorite activities is a way to show you care. It may even inspire new ideas and adventures. As you grow and discover new favorites, keep in mind that whom you spend your time with is more important than what you're doing.

Embrace your similarities and celebrate your differences! Laugh with each other and prioritize your friendship whenever you have the chance.

YOU'RE MY FAVORITE FRIEND

About the Author

Katelyn Cole is a content creator and passionate book lover based in Texas. A former elementary teacher with a background in primary and upper elementary grades, Special Education, ESL, and Gifted and Talented, Katelyn now uses her passion for education and literacy to inspire people of all ages to reignite their love of reading. She started her online community, **The Bookcase Beauty**, as a way to find and connect with other book lovers. Since the beginning, she has now grown her audience on Instagram to over 96,000 followers and expanded her content to include home and lifestyle content that support the bookish life! Katelyn is driven by the mission to use her platform to inspire community and connection with others. To learn more, visit *www.thebookcasebeauty.com* and @**bookcasebeauty** on Instagram.

BETTER DAY BOOKS®
HAPPY • CREATIVE • CURATED

Business is personal at Better Day Books. We were founded on the belief that all people are creative and that making things by hand is inherently good for us. It's important to us that you know how much we appreciate your support. The book you are holding in your hands was crafted with the artistic passion of the author and brought to life by a team of wildly enthusiastic creatives who believed it could inspire you. If it did, please drop us a line and let us know about it. Connect with us on Instagram, post a photo of your art, and let us know what other creative pursuits you are interested in learning about. It all matters to us. You're kind of a big deal.

it's a good day to have a better day!®

www.betterdaybooks.com
better_day_books